Night-Night, Knight

And Other Poems

Read it together

It's never too early to share books with children. Reading together is a wonderful way for your child to enjoy books and stories — and learn to read!

One of the most important ways of helping your child learn to read is by reading aloud — either rereading their favorite books, or getting to know new ones.

Encourage your child to join in with the reading in every possible way. They may be able to talk about the pictures, point to the words, take over parts of the reading, or retell the story afterward.

With books they know well, children can try reading to you. Don't worry if the words aren't always the same as the words on the page.

If they are reading and get stuck on a word, show them how to guess what it says by:
* looking at the pictures
* looking at the letter the word begins with
* reading the rest of the sentence and coming back to it.

Always help them out if they get really stuck or tired.

> *I am running in a circle and my feet are getting sore, and my head is sp—*

I am running in a circle
and my feet are getting sore,
and my head is
spi...

> **If I cover the ending, what does it say?**

> **Morning" and "warning"— they sound the same.**

> **"Awake" and "shake"— can you find any more words that rhyme?**

Sometimes you can help children look more closely at the actual words and letters. See if they can find words they recognize, or letters from their name. Help them write some of the words they know.

> **Do you know my favorite? The naughty one that says "I won't."**

Talk about books with them and discuss the stories and pictures. Compare new books with ones they already know.

We hope you enjoy reading this book together.

For Caroline, Kaz, and Clare
S. H.

Poems chosen by Michael Rosen
All uncredited poems are traditional or anonymously authored.
Illustrations copyright © 1998 by Sue Heap
Introductory and concluding notes © 1998 by CLPE/L B Southwark

Second U.S. edition in this form 1999

Library of Congress Catalog Card Number 98-88075

ISBN 0-7636-0856-4

10 9 8 7 6 5 4

Printed in Hong Kong

Candlewick Press
2067 Massachusetts Avenue
Cambridge, Massachusetts 02140

The editor and publisher gratefully acknowledge permission to reproduce the following copyright material:

John Agard: "So-So Joe" from No Hickory, No Dickory, No Dock published by Viking 1991 and "Where Does Laughter Begin?" from Laughter Is an Egg published by Viking 1990, reprinted by kind permission of John Agard c/o Caroline Sheldon Literary Agency. Tony Bradman: "I Can Put My Socks On" from A Kiss on the Nose, reprinted by permission of William Heinemann. Richard Edwards: "How?" from The Word Party published by Puffin 1987, reprinted by permission of the author. Eleanor Farjeon: "Cats" from The Children's Bells, reprinted by permission of David Higham Associates. Michelle Magorian: "I Won't" from Waiting for My Shorts to Dry published by Viking Kestrel 1989 © Michelle Magorian 1989, reprinted by permission of Frederick Warne & Co. Spike Milligan: "Today I Saw a Little Worm" © Spike Milligan 1959, 1961, 1963, reprinted by permission of Spike Milligan Productions Ltd.

Grace Nichols: "Granny, Granny, Please Comb My Hair" from Come On into My Tropical Garden published by A & C Black, reprinted by permission of Curtis Brown Ltd., on behalf of Grace Nichols © 1988. Jack Prelutsky: "I Am Running in a Circle" from New Kid on the Block, reprinted by permission of William Heinemann Ltd. Clive Sansom: "The Dustman" from Speech Rhymes, reprinted by permission of A & C Black Ltd. Ian Serraillier: "The Tickle Rhyme" from The Monster Horse © 1950 published by Oxford University Press, reprinted by permission of Anne Serraillier.

While every effort has been made to obtain permission, there may still be cases in which we have failed to trace a copyright holder, and we would like to apologize for any apparent negligence.

Night-Night, Knight
And Other Poems

chosen by
Michael Rosen

illustrated by
Sue Heap

CANDLEWICK PRESS

So-So Joe

So-So Joe
de so-so man
wore a so-so suit
with a so-so shoe.
So-So Joe
de so-so man
lived in a so-so house
with a so-so view.
And when you asked So-So Joe
de so-so man
How do you do?
So-So Joe
de so-so man
would say to you:
Just so-so
Nothing new.

John Agard

Fire

Fire! Fire!
said Mrs. Dyer;
Where? Where?
said Mrs. Dare;
Up the town,
said Mrs. Brown;
Any damage?
said Mrs. Gamage;
None at all,
said Mrs. Hall.

The Dustman

Every Thursday morning,
Before you're quite awake,
Without the slightest warning
The house begins to shake
With a Biff! . . . Bang!
Biff! Bang! Bash!

It's the dustman, who begins
(Bang! . . . Crash!)
To empty both the bins
Of their rubbish and their ash,
With a Biff! . . . Bang!
Biff! Bang! Bash!

Clive Sansom

The Key of the Kingdom

This is the key of the kingdom:
In that kingdom is a city,
In that city is a town,
In that town there is a street,
In that street there winds a lane,
In that lane there is a yard,
In that yard there is a house,
In that house there waits a room,
In that room there is a bed,
On that bed there is a basket,
A basket of flowers.

Flowers in the basket,
Basket on the bed,
Bed in the room,
Room in the house,
House in the weedy yard,
Yard in the winding lane,
Lane in the broad street,
Street in the high town,
Town in the city,
City in the kingdom:
This is the key of the kingdom.

Lane

kingdom

Our City

Our house

Our yard

r town

Our room

Street

Granny, Granny, Please Comb My Hair

Granny, Granny,
please comb my hair
you always take your time
you always take such care

You put me to sit on a cushion
between your knees
you rub a little coconut oil
parting gentle as a breeze

Mommy, Mommy,
she's always in a hurry-hurry
rush
she pulls my hair
sometimes she tugs

But, Granny,
you have all the time in the world
and when you're finished
you always turn my head and say,
"Now who's a nice girl."

Grace Nichols

After a Bath

After my bath
I try, try, try
to wipe myself
till I'm dry, dry, dry.

Hands to wipe
and fingers and toes
and two wet legs
and a shiny nose.

Just think how much
less time I'd take
if I were a dog
and could shake, shake, shake.

Aileen Fisher

I Can Put My Socks On

I can put my socks on,
I can find my vest,
I can put my pants on—
I can't do the rest.

Tony Bradman

There Was a Young Lady Named Maggie
There was a young lady named Maggie,
Whose dog was enormous and shaggy.
    The front end of him
     Looked vicious and grim,
But the back end was friendly and waggy.

A Cheerful Old Bear at the Zoo
A cheerful old bear at the zoo,
Could always find something to do.
    When it bored him to go
     On a walk to and fro,
He reversed it and walked fro and to.

There Was a Young Farmer of Leeds

There was a young farmer of Leeds,
Who swallowed six packets of seeds.
    It soon came to pass
    He was covered with grass,
And he couldn't sit down for the weeds.

There Was a Young Man of Devizes

There was a young man of Devizes,
Whose ears were of different sizes.
    One was so small
    It was no use at all,
But the other was huge and won prizes.

I Won't

I won't, no, I won't, no, I won't do that.
I don't want to, I don't have to,
No, I won't wear that hat.

I hate it, yes, I hate it, yes, I hate, hate, hate.
You can't make me, I don't want to,
I don't care if we are late.

Yes, I'm naughty, yes, I'm naughty,
Yes, I know, know, know.
But I won't wear that hat
So it's No! No! No!

Michelle Magorian

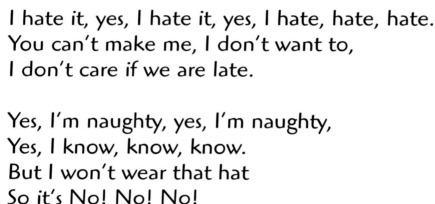

Overheard on a Salt Marsh

Nymph, nymph, what are your beads?
        Green glass, goblin. Why do you
        stare at them?
Give them me.
        No.
Give them me. Give them me.
        No.
Then I will howl all night in the reeds,
Lie in the mud and howl for them.
        Goblin, why do you love them so?
They are better than stars or water,
Better than voices of winds that sing,
Better than any man's fair daughter,
Your green glass beads on a silver ring.

        Hush, I stole them out of
        the moon.
Give me your beads, I desire them.
        No.
I will howl in a deep lagoon
For your green glass beads, I love them so.
Give them me. Give them.
        No.

Harold Munro

Swan, Swim over the Sea
Swan, swim over the sea.
Swim, swan, swim!
Swan, swim back again.
Well swum, swan!

Night-Night, Knight
"Night-night, Knight," said one Knight
to the other Knight the other night.
"Night-night, Knight."

Peter Piper Picked a Peck of Pickled Pepper

Peter Piper picked a peck of pickled pepper,
A peck of pickled pepper Peter Piper picked.
If Peter Piper picked a peck of pickled pepper,
Where's the peck of pickled pepper Peter Piper picked?

Cats

Cats sleep
Anywhere,
Any table,
Any chair,
Top of piano,
Window ledge,
In the middle,
On the edge,
Open drawer,
Empty shoe,
Anybody's
Lap will do,
Fitted in a
Cardboard box,
In the cupboard
With your frocks—
Anywhere!
They don't care!
Cats sleep
Anywhere.

Eleanor Farjeon

The Kitten
The trouble with a kitten is
THAT
Eventually it becomes a
CAT.

Ogden Nash

NURSERY CRIMES by Michael Rosen

Hush-a-Bye, Gravy, on the Treetop

Hush-a-bye, gravy, on the treetop,
When the wind blows, the ladle will rock;
When the bough breaks, the ladle will fall,
Down will come gravy, ladle and all.

Humpty Dumpty Sat on the Wall

Humpty Dumpty sat on the wall,
Humpty Dumpty had a great fall;
All the king's horses and all the king's men
Trod on him.

Hey Diddle, Diddle

Hey diddle, diddle,
The cat and the fiddle,
The cow jumped over the moon;
The little dog laughed
To see such fun,
And the dish ran away with the cookies.

Today I Saw a Little Worm

Today I saw a little worm
Wriggling on his belly.
Perhaps he'd like to come inside
And see what's on the telly.

Spike Milligan

Who's That Tickling My Back?
"Who's that tickling my back?"
Said the wall.
"Me," said the caterpillar.
"I'm learning to crawl."   *Ian Serraillier*

Where Does Laughter Begin?

Does it start in your head
and spread to your toe?

Does it start in your cheeks
and grow downward so
till your knees feel weak?

Does it start with a tickle
in your tummy so
till you want to jump right out

of all your skin
Or does laughter simply begin

with your mouth?

John Agard

Questions at Night

Why
Is the sky?

What starts the thunder overhead?
Who makes the crashing noise?
Are the angels falling out of bed?
Are they breaking all their toys?

Why does the sun go down so soon?
Why do the night clouds crawl
Hungrily up to the new-laid moon
And swallow it, shell and all?

If there's a Bear among the stars,
As all the people say,
Won't he jump over those pasture bars
And drink up the Milky Way?

Does every star that happens to fall
Turn into a firefly?
Can't it ever get back to Heaven at all?
And why
Is the sky?

Louis Untermeyer

How?

How did the sun get up in the sky?
—A billy goat tossed it up too high,
Said my uncle.

How did the stars get up there too?
—They're sparks from the thunder horse's shoe,
Said my uncle.

And tell me about the moon as well.
—The moon jumped out of an oyster shell,
Said my uncle.

And how did the oceans get so deep?
—I'll tell you tomorrow. Now, go to sleep,
Said my uncle.

Richard Edwards

Silverly

Silverly,
    Silverly
Over the
    Trees,
The moon drifts
    By on a
Runaway
    Breeze.

Dozily,
    Dozily
Deep in her
    Bed,
A little girl
    Dreams with the
Moon in her
    Head.

Dennis Lee

Read it again

Learn a poem
Children can learn a favorite poem by heart if they hear it and read it again and again. They might be encouraged to act it out for you with simple props, or tape it with sound effects and simple musical instruments.

The other was huge and won prizes.

"Who's that tickling my back?" Said the wall.

"Me," said the caterpillar. . . .

Play reading
It can be fun to read a poem by passing it between adult and child, like reading a play. Good poems for this are "Overheard on a Salt Marsh," "Who's That Tickling My Back?," "Fire," and "How?"

Collecting poems
Your child can select a favorite poem to illustrate, using a large sheet of paper. Your child could copy out the poem, perhaps with your help, and stick it on the wall.

A cheerful old bear at the ZOO Could always find something to do: when it bored him to go On a walk to and fro He reversed it and walked fro and to.

Make a collection
You could also put together a collection of your child's favorite poems and rhymes in a little book. These can be illustrated and read time and time again.

Play the poem game

You and your child can play the poem game and test your knowledge of the poems. Take turns choosing a square and answering the question. You can check the answers by looking back through the book.

Reading Together

The Reading Together series is divided into four levels—starting with red, then on to yellow, blue, and finally green. The six books in each level offer children varied experiences of reading. There are stories, poems, rhymes and songs, traditional tales, and information books to choose from.

Accompanying the series is the *Reading Together Parents' Handbook,* which looks at all the different ways children learn to read and explains how *your* help can really make a difference!